Original title:
The Sound of Watering

Copyright © 2025 Creative Arts Management OÜ
All rights reserved.

Author: Nora Sinclair
ISBN HARDBACK: 978-1-80581-831-1
ISBN PAPERBACK: 978-1-80581-358-3
ISBN EBOOK: 978-1-80581-831-1

Streams of Satisfied Soil

A gurgle here, a splash over there,
Dancing droplets in the humid air.
Plants cheer up with a soggy song,
Roots wiggle under, where they belong.

The cactus sighs, the ferns start to twist,
Every leaf waving, can't resist.
Laughing as puddles form a parade,
Happy little sprouts in a watery cascade.

Fluid Whispers of Awakening Life

A trickle laughs as it tickles a rock,
While daisies nodding, do a little walk.
The clouds conspire with a chuckle and grin,
As sunflowers spin, letting the party begin!

Worms peek out, they're ready to groove,
Mud masks on, in the rain they'll move.
Each droplet's a dancer, an acrobat too,
Ballet on grass, who knew they could do?

Life's Elixir for Dreaming Green

With a splash, plants bounce in delight,
While carrots chuckle at their watery plight.
Lavender leans in for a fragrant sip,
And leafy greens join in the fun as they flip.

Showering joy like a rainmaker's charm,
While roots are giggling, it's quite the alarm.
Petals prance, they're feeling so spry,
As droplets tickle and the moss waves goodbye.

Vibrations of Verdant Vitality

Listen closely, can you hear them cheer?
The little sprouts whisper, "Bring us more here!"
The grapevines tangle in a bubbly spree,
While the daisies dip in, dancing for free.

With each little splash, a joke takes flight,
They plot wild capers in the cool moonlight.
Every leaf giggles, swaying with flair,
In the garden's party, there's plenty to share.

Ripples in Silence

In the garden green and bright,
A hose went rogue, what a sight!
Spraying plants all willy-nilly,
Making frogs dance, oh so silly.

The watercress did tap step dance,
While daisies giggled, took a chance.
A puddle formed, a wiggly mirth,
As snails spun tales of mossy girth.

Liquid Whispers

A droplet teetered, ready to fall,
On a leaf, it held a ball.
With a splash, that droplet flew,
And missed the pond; oh, what a boo!

'The fish are grumpy,' said a crow,
'You missed the party, don't you know?'
While crickets laughed, joined the game,
In this watery world, no one's to blame.

Symphony of the Sprouts

Water tunes on sprightly leaves,
A frog conducts, the garden weaves.
Tulips sway to a bubbly beat,
And broccoli shakes its little feet.

The carrots hum, a rooty choir,
As daisies twirl, they never tire.
The rain drops join, all shapes and sizes,
This leafy shindig yields surprises!

Echoes of Graceful Rain

Little drizzles fall like jokes,
On umbrellas worn by folks.
The puddles laugh with a splishy sound,
While boots make friends with muddy ground.

Clouds giggle softly, a skyward cheer,
As rain dances down like a party cheer.
The world's a stage for droplets grand,
In this mosaic made by hand.

Fresh Awakening in Droplets

Tiny pearls fall from above,
Making plants dance, it's love.
They giggle as they soak it in,
Nature's bath, let the fun begin.

Splashes here, a splash there,
The flowers wear a soggy glare.
In puddles, frogs start their songs,
Even snails join in, singing along.

Resonance of Nature's Hydration

Listen close to the drip-drop sound,
Where thirsty roots poke underground.
It's a concert of quench, a splashy feat,
As droplets tap dance on the street.

Raindrops jaunt on leaves so bright,
Tickling flowers with pure delight.
While worms do their wiggle in the mud,
Nature's own dance, a joyful flood.

Swells of Green Hope

Joyful seeds burst forth with cheer,
As they sip on rainwater here.
Sprouts stretch tall to greet the sun,
It's a race to grow, oh what fun!

With every sip, they laugh and play,
In the warm embrace of a sunny ray.
Watch the buds bounce, it's quite a sight,
Nature's party is out tonight!

Rivulets of Promise

A trickle runs, a watery tease,
It whispers softly to the trees.
"Oh hush now, don't go too fast!
We need to sip this joy to last!"

Catch some drops in a playful dance,
Wiggly worms join in the chance.
Each rivulet flows with giddy glee,
Quenching dreams for all to see.

Echoes of Earth's Thirst

In the garden, droplets play,
Tickling leaves in a ballet.
Worms wiggle, tap dance with glee,
While flowers giggle, feeling free.

A hose debates, it beats the heat,
Dancing wildly, oh what a feat!
The garden hose, a serpent bright,
Sprays the cat, oh what a sight!

Rippled Remembrances

The puddles pop like bubble gum,
As frogs croak tunes, they strum and hum.
Ducks parade in feathery lines,
Quacking jokes, oh how the sun shines!

Sprinklers spin, a water show,
Hopping through streams, jumping to and fro.
Never a dull moment, it seems,
In the dance of drops and sunny beams!

The Language of Liquid

Raindrops chatter, a silly choir,
Moisture whispers, sparks of desire.
Leaves are laughing, drinking up cheer,
With each splash, the giggles draw near.

A bucket rolls, joins in the fun,
Its handle sways, it's become a gun!
Shooting water with silly glee,
Making mischief, just you and me!

Trickle Through Time

A trickle chats down the garden path,
Providing clues to nature's math.
It's a race, who splashes best?
The frog leaps high, beats all the rest.

Gnomes take bets on who will dry,
While clouds above puff out a sigh.
Time ticks by in a fluid swirl,
Embroidery of wet dreams unfurl!

Symphony of the Thirsty Soil

Beneath the sun, the ground does plead,
With crackles and pops—a thirsty creed.
It drinks with glee, a jovial fuss,
As roots put on their dancing shoes.

A tap-tap-tap, the rain's a tease,
Each droplet brings a giggling breeze.
The plants sway left, then right they go,
In this odd ballet, they steal the show.

Dancing Streams of Rejuvenation

Little streams prance, they giggle and gleam,
Waltzing through rocks, they plot and scheme.
They splash on leaves, in joyful rebellion,
Making muddy puddles—their true million.

With every twist, they make signs of cheer,
Whispering secrets only fish can hear.
And frogs leap in like they own the scene,
Croaking along like they're part of the dream.

Rhythmic Embrace of Nature

Nature claps as raindrops fall,
Dancing on soil—what a ball!
The worms wiggle in pure delight,
Signing autographs beneath starlight.

A soggy cat comes out to play,
Chasing drops in a very strange way.
The puddles giggle, "Catch us if you can!"
But the cat slips down—what a funny plan!

Liquid Chords in a Verdant Realm

In the garden, a chorus sings,
Of raindrops plunking like vibrant strings.
The daisies bow, the grasses sway,
As nature's band begins to play.

Olive trees sway with limbs so bold,
Even the daisies join the fold.
The earth takes a sip—a big, hearty gulp,
And the hiccup echoes like a joyous yelp.

Tinkling Water and Tender Blossoms

A gentle splash, a giggle near,
Dancing droplets, what a cheer!
Plants are laughing, what a sight,
Tickled leaves in morning light.

With tiny waves, they play a tune,
Sipping sunshine, under the moon.
Petals prancing, roots at play,
Joyful blooms in grand ballet.

Each sprout sings, with glee and grace,
Watering can, a funny face!
Wobbly stems in rhythm sway,
Nature's chuckle, brightens day.

With every drop, a tale unfolds,
In this garden, humor molds.
Tiny frogs join in the fun,
Laughing leaves, oh what a run!

The Gentle Flow of Growth

A little trickle, a sneaky stream,
Making puddles, like a dream.
Sprouts twirl and whirl with delight,
In this water dance, what a sight!

One little drop, a prankster bold,
Tugs at roots, stories told.
Hoses giggle, splashing around,
Funny faces, laughter found.

Potted plants with a wink and grin,
In a soaked game, where to begin?
Their leafy laughter fills the air,
Dancing droplets, light as a flare.

With each gush, a giddy cheer,
Quenching roots with splashes near.
Garden parties, all around,
Watering whimsies, joy is found!

Cadence of Quenching Life

A sprinkle here, a drizzle there,
Tiny dancers in the air.
The garden hums a silly song,
With water's rhythm, they dance along.

Each little raindrop has a joke,
Bouncing off, a wet-spun cloak.
Plants in stitches, leaning close,
Sharing secrets with each dose.

As canisters clink in silly lines,
Hoses giggle with twisted vines.
Every bloom has a quirky plan,
In the ballet of the watering can.

Roots all wave, in giddy bends,
With every splash, the fun never ends.
Nature chuckles, what a delight,
Quenching laughter in pure sunlight!

Harmony in a Silken Stream

A ribbon flows with giggles bright,
Dripping joy in morning light.
Leaves wiggle with a joking tease,
As the stream whispers with such ease.

Tiny hands with can in tow,
Spraying rain like a garden show.
Frogs leap high with splish and splash,
Nature's laughter in a flash.

In puddles deep, the fish do wiggle,
As if they're caught in a silly giggle.
Water meets root in a warm embrace,
Filling the garden with smiles in place.

Every drop's a friendly tease,
Quenching thirst with style and ease.
In a lush parade, all sounds align,
Harmony flows, just divine!

Cascading Notes of Renewal

Tiny droplets dance in the air,
They twirl and spin without a care.
In garden hats, the plants rejoice,
As every leaf hums in a voice.

The hose is tangled, what a mess,
I wiggle and squirm, oh what duress!
Water's falling, splashing spree,
It's like a party, just for me!

Buckets and spouts, all in a race,
I chase the water like a wild chase.
The sprinklers gossip, spin and whirl,
Making the roses giggle and twirl.

With every splash, a new surprise,
The veggies gleam like jeweled eyes.
They thank me with a leafy cheer,
For every miss, their fun is clear!

Fluid Caresses on Garden Beds

My hose looks like it's lost its way,
It spirals, twists—oh what a play!
Small puddles form, like little jokes,
As I chaseafter, laughing with folks.

The daisies dance with graceful glee,
While muddy boots try to flee.
A cheeky robin steals a sip,
While I'm caught in a water drip.

With every gush, a playful splash,
My gloves are soaked, oh what a clash!
The sun peeks out, it winks at me,
As plants throw a party, wild and free.

Watering cans in a twirling spree,
I'm drenched, but the blooms are happy.
Their laughter echoes through the sun,
As I drip dance 'til the job is done!

Delicate Drizzles of Delight

Tiny streams trickle down the lane,
Each plight of mine is their gained fame.
My aim is true, but aim is shot,
The flowers giggle, they plot a lot.

With buckets in hand, I'm quite the sight,
Each step I take is a clumsy fright.
The veggies chuckle, they know my game,
As I splash around without a shame.

Little critters watch from afar,
Snickering softly, 'Oh, there's our star!'
With each passing drop, a merry dance,
Nature's humor in a frolicsome chance.

When I finally trip, a grand display,
The plants rejoice, "Hip hip hooray!"
They soak me back with a little rain,
And everyone laughs—oh, what a gain!

Trickle of Life's Rebirth

A hose unwinds in wild delight,
Spraying arcs like a knight's fight.
I'm drenched to the skin, it's quite absurd,
As laughing blooms whisper every word.

With every squirt, their cheers rise high,
While I fumble in warmth, oh me, oh my!
The pests flee from this watery storm,
As I create a liquid art form.

Amidst the giggles, I spill and trip,
Water flows like it's on a rip.
Leaves wiggle, embracing the froth,
While I rename this—a hydrous sloth!

As I splash about, I take a bow,
The garden claims me, I can't say how.
Each drop a chuckle, each spray a thrill,
In this circus of water, I get my fill!

Refrain of Sprouting Splendor

Little droplets dance and play,
Sipping greens in bright array.
With a comedic splash and flip,
Plants perform their drinky dip.

Laughter bubbles, glee takes flight,
Roots wiggling with sheer delight.
They sway and jiggle, oh what a sight!
Who knew veggies could be so bright?

Choreography of Clear Currents

The garden's stage is set just right,
With hose-turned-dancer in the light.
Each squirt and spray, a sprightly jig,
Making veggies hop, oh so big!

Tiny sprouts with rhythm in their stems,
Turning stalactites into gems.
A tango of water, soil, and fun,
Nature's party, oh, we've just begun!

Trail of Tapping Thirst

Pitter-patter on the ground,
Silly sounds all around.
Roots tap dance in sweet delight,
Quenching thirst, what a sight!

Drip, drop, giggles in the air,
Nature's laughter everywhere.
Plants with cups, like kids at play,
Sipping sunshine all the day!

Serenade of Soaked Roots

Underneath the leafy crown,
Roots are singing, never frown.
With a splash, and a playful cheer,
Guzzling water, loud and clear.

Each sip a note, a melody,
In the garden's symphony.
Seeds sprouting jokes, in rows they stand,
Nature's humor, oh so grand!

A Ballet of Moisture and Growth

In a garden full of glee,
The plants all dance in sync,
With droplets tapping feet,
While worms clumsily clink.

Sprinklers twirl like dancers do,
With water pirouettes,
The daisies throw a little shade,
And make a joke on pets.

The tomatoes giggle red,
As raindrops splash around,
"Don't drown us!" they all shout,
While puddles spin and bound.

Each leaf a bit soggy,
Yet happy as can be,
The funny splashy ballet,
Makes nature laugh with glee.

Streamed Harmonies in the Landscape

Raindrops plop like little notes,
A symphony begins,
Each splash a happy chorus,
Where mischief always wins.

The river sings a merry tune,
As frogs add to the beat,
With bubbles popping giggly,
They dance upon their feet.

Puddles hold grand concerts,
With splashes as the bass,
And fireflies flutter 'round,
In this joyful water race!

The grass shakes off its song,
With laughter in the breeze,
As nature's concert plays along,
In easy, silly tease.

The Thrum of Rejuvenation

A drip, a drop, a playful slosh,
The thirsty plants rejoice,
Each leaf a cheerful face,
Singing with a bubbly voice.

The flowers flash their petals wide,
As droplets bounce and gleam,
"Hey look, it's raining again!"
They giggle with a dream.

The lawn mowers take a break,
For they might get a drink,
While ants parade in rubber boots,
All marching with a wink.

When water pours a happy mix,
The garden throws a bash,
With laughter in the raindrops,
And mud that makes a splash!

Waters Unfold the Emerald Tapestry

In drizzles soft and squishy,
The plants wear hats of dew,
While puddles form like mirrors,
Reflecting skies so blue.

The daisies play peek-a-boo,
As snails go sliding by,
Whispers in wet harmony,
Underneath the playful sky.

Oh, how the blades sway gently,
To the rhythm of the rain,
With critters jumping joyfully,
Demanding more to gain.

The landscape sings an emerald tune,
With giggles on the rise,
As nature's light and laughter bloom,
Beneath the happy skies.

Sprinkles of Hope in Every Drop

Tiny droplets falling down,
Like little jesters in a gown.
They dance and bounce on thirsty ground,
Whispering secrets, giggles abound.

Curly leaves look up in cheer,
"Is that a shower we can hear?"
Potatoes grinning, roots all a-jump,
Wishing for rain to give them a thump.

Clouds above all puffed up nice,
Playing peekaboo, oh what a slice!
Together they plot a splashy scheme,
To keep the garden dancing in a dream.

So here we stand with watering cans,
Pretending to be rain, not just mere fans.
Winking at flowers, urging them to grow,
In this silly dance, let the laughter flow!

Nature's Nurturing Whisper

A gentle drip, a little plop,
The flowers giggle, they just won't stop.
"Hey buddy, catch a little shower!"
As grass turns green, they bloom with power.

The daisies sway with a cheeky grin,
While shy moss blushes just beneath the din.
"More love please, don't hold back!"
As mud pies form on the grassy track.

Rabbits hop, they twist and whirl,
Chasing droplets with a playful twirl.
The thirsty trees all stretch and yawn,
In this moist world, every sigh's a song.

With each splash, the world wakes wide,
Grinning at puddles, take a wild ride.
Nature winks with every drip,
In this party, let's take a dip!

Harmonious Flow of Verdant Dreams

Raindrops tapping on the roof,
Like tiny dancers in a goof.
The garden claps its leafy hands,
As laughter frolics through the lands.

Petals stretch like sleepy cats,
Awake to laughter, no room for bats.
Wiggly worms join in the fun,
As raindrops shine like everyone.

Bright cucumbers wear a funny hat,
While carrots wiggle in a spat.
The stream joins in with a bubbling tune,
While goldfish wear a shiny balloon.

Each drop's a joke, a playful tease,
Turning gardens into a breeze.
So grab your boots, splash around,
In this merry mirth, joy is found!

Liquid Lullabies in the Orchard

A splash of joy in morning light,
Apple blossoms dance with delight.
"C'mon, give us more, we want a show!"
The cherries chuckle, all in a row.

Hoses swirl like ribbons bright,
Spouting giggles, what a sight!
Grapes huddle close, forming a throng,
Singing silly tunes, all day long.

Melons roll with a jolly plop,
Bouncing like they just can't stop.
Spilling laughter with every drop,
While bumblebees hop and bop.

Every squirt, a splash of cheer,
In this orchard, love draws near.
Together we laugh and share the tears,
In this garden of joy, let's shift our gears!

Nature's Rejuvenating Thrum

Little droplets dance and splash,
They play a game, oh what a bash!
Jumping here, then splashing there,
Puddles giggle, who needs a chair?

In the garden, flowers cheer,
With every drop, they draw near.
The sun smiles down, a warm embrace,
While worms take swims in their own race!

Bees hum tunes, a buzzing choir,
While snails slow down, their pace doesn't tire.
With every sip, plants grow so spry,
Their leafy limbs wave up to the sky.

Rain boots on, we splash about,
In muddy patches, there's no doubt.
Nature's rhythm, a crazy show,
Water's tune makes everything grow!

Tones of the Thirst Quencher

A canister clinks, an orchestra's start,
Grass sways in rhythm, it's nature's art.
Squirrels grab snacks, they scurry so fast,
While raindrops join in—what a blast!

Hoses wiggle like snakes at play,
Spraying the flowers in a colorful spray.
Kids shriek in joy, dashing through streams,
Turning the leaks into wild, wet dreams.

Frogs croak along, a frothy refrain,
As butterflies dance in the light summer rain.
The world is a stage, each critter a star,
With every wet note, we giggle from afar.

Time for a break, grab a cold drink,
Watch as the daisies begin to wink.
Who knew this tune would bring such delight?
Watering fun, oh what a sight!

Bursting Buds and Liquid Melodies

Sprinklers whirl like a playful breeze,
Dancing droplets up to the trees.
Rabbits hop by, shaking with glee,
They find every puddle as fun as can be.

Garden gnomes join in the fun,
Drenched in laughter, soaking up sun.
A flower's giggle, so sweet and bright,
As bees buzz along, their dance a delight.

Joyful plants stretch, reaching for air,
While thirsty worms wiggle without a care.
Each petal shimmies, a vibrant display,
Under sparkling skies, they love to play!

The laughter of nature, a wild, fresh song,
Makes watering time feel like a party all day long.
So grab your friends, let's have a whirl,
Watering magic, let the fun unfurl!

Cadence of Nature's Quench

The bucket tumbles, hits the ground,
Splashes echo, a joyful sound.
Creatures skitter, in puddles they leap,
While flowers giggle, their roots in a heap.

A hose takes flight, wriggles with glee,
Like a dance-off for the ants, can't you see?
They twirl and twist, so spry and free,
While puddles become a grand jubilee.

Laughter erupts, it's a watery spree,
As squirrels make mischief, climbing a tree.
Each droplet counts, a comedic beat,
In nature's rhythm, it's all so sweet!

Now let's rejoice with each splash and cheer,
For every little drop brings the joy near.
So grab your galoshes, don't forget your hat,
In the watering ballet, let's all have a chat!

Cascading Nourishment

A rubber duck floats in my pot,
While daisies dance, oh what a thought!
A sprinkler sprays, a water ballet,
Plants laughing loud in the sun's warm ray.

Squeaky shoes on wet grass slip,
With each drip drop, the gnomes do skip.
Frogs in tuxedos begin to croon,
Singing along to a jazzy tune.

Birds hop in puddles, doing the twist,
Chickens do cha-chas, they can't resist.
Worms wiggle out, they join the parade,
Marching in rhythm, oh, what a charade!

So grab your hose and let's have a show,
The garden's a stage, it's time for the flow.
With giggles and splashes, the day rolls along,
Join in the fun, dance to the song!

A Dance of Refreshing Streams

A tiny stream does a little jig,
While ants don hats, the only gig.
With splashes and bubbles, they shimmy and sway,
Leaves clapping hands, they join the fray.

The goldfish wear ties, they swim in a line,
While frogs leap and croak, keeping it fine.
Splashing each other, oh what a sight,
As sunbeams perform with pure delight.

A rabbit hops in, twirls round the muck,
Searching for carrots, oh, what a luck!
Puddles reflect a real party scene,
Nature's dance floor, all shiny and green.

So grab your boots, don't forget the fun,
When water plays, we all come undone.
With laughter and splashes, let this day gleam,
Join in the dance, let's live the dream!

The Timeless Song of Soil

Beneath the ground, where jokes are made,
Earthworms chuckle in manure shade.
Giggly roots stretch, there's no need to scoff,
They wiggle with joy, never take it off!

Raindrops play tunes on leaves like drums,
While daisies hum softly, oh how it strums!
The soil shakes gently, a giggling lump,
As critters unite with a celebratory thump.

Silly bugs tap dance with all of their might,
In muddy ballrooms, beneath moonlight.
Their legs move swiftly, full of delight,
With each little puddle, they twirl and ignite.

So let us all laugh at the dirt and grime,
Where nature's humor flows just like thyme.
Raise a glass to the soil, and dance the night away,
With earthy laughter, let's seize the day!

Whispering Waters

A brook gossips secrets, oh, what a tease,
It tickles the toes of the swaying trees.
Fish make a splash in a belly flop spree,
While the frogs on the bank sing in harmony.

A snail in a top hat takes a regal stroll,
While puddles reflect a synchronized roll.
Bubble-blowing ducks have a giggle fit,
Making sure laughter is infinite!

With watercress waltzing in sunny ballet,
And moss-covered rocks showing off in their way.
It's a slippery party, the frogs steal the show,
As wise old turtles say, "Take it slow!"

So come take a dip in this merry brigade,
Let laughter flow free as we all serenade.
With whispers of water, let joy be our tune,
Embrace the hilarity, morning to noon!

Melodies of the Moist Earth

The droplets dance upon the ground,
Creating rhythms, quite profound.
Trees join in with rustling glee,
A symphony from nature's spree.

Worms wiggle to the drumming beat,
While daisies sway, oh what a treat!
The puddles splash with cheerful tones,
Even the grass hums in joyful moans.

Bees buzz in harmony, quite bold,
Joining the chorus, a story told.
Each sprout learns a catchy rhyme,
In the playful midst of verdant prime.

As rainbows arch, they clap along,
In this garden where all belong.
The melodies of earth's embrace,
Leave us giggling in this space.

Echoes in the Garden

Oh, listen close, the plants can sing,
When raindrops fall, oh, what a fling!
Tomatoes chuckle as they grow,
While carrots dance in rows all aglow.

Petunias gossip, rustle their leaves,
Thrilled by dribbles as the earth sheaves.
Basil does a jolly jig,
Even the radish gets in the gig.

With splashes bright, they make quite noise,
Like a party of leafy girls and boys.
Puddle-jumpers leap with zest,
Creating echoes of nature's best.

Every sigh and splash declares,
In this garden, laughter shares.
A joyful jest, a leafy cheer,
With every droplet, love draws near.

Chiming Raindrops on Leaves

Raindrops tumble, tickling trees,
Chiming softly in the breeze.
Leaves giggle, in a wild sway,
Singing tunes of play all day.

Branches tap their tiny toes,
While lily pads twirl in rows.
Flowers laugh, twirling in spins,
Celebrating each drippy din.

Every puddle's a stage set,
For frogs to croak, a croaky duet.
Squirrels slide with fuzzy flair,
Join the rhythm, light as air.

In this garden, joy is clear,
A raindrop playdate, never fear.
With every plop, a hearty cheer,
A concert bright, all we hold dear.

Lullaby of New Beginnings

The sky weeps softly, a gentle start,
Bringing life, warming every heart.
Sprouts whisper secrets, waking from dreams,
In the hush of dappled moonbeams.

Little seedlings stretch with grace,
Relishing each nurturing trace.
Pansies peek out, their colors bright,
In giggles shared, a pure delight.

The air is filled with jubilant sighs,
As clouds play tag in cotton skies.
Every droplet a tender kiss,
Bringing forth life, oh what bliss.

Beneath the surface, joy abounds,
As laughter flows from bubbling grounds.
With the dawn, new laughs commence,
In this halcyon of innocence.

Humming Springs

In the garden, gurgles play,
A dance of droplets, bright as day.
Flowers giggle, petals sway,
Like little kids at a grand ballet.

Water's pranks, oh what a tease,
Tickling roots and swaying trees.
With every splash, their laughter frees,
Nature's joy takes such ease.

Bubbles pop with silly sounds,
Joyous leaps, as joy abounds.
Leaping frogs in happy rounds,
The merry scene of happy grounds.

So come and join this frothy fun,
With every stream, a wild run.
In this world, we're all just spun,
Chasing drops, oh what a pun!

Raindrops' Rhapsody

Tapping on rooftops, a jolly tune,
A rhythm that makes the flowers swoon.
Puddles giggle, reflecting the moon,
Under the sky, life finds its boon.

Jumpy drops in tap-dance shoes,
Sashay around without a bruise.
Nature's song has playful clues,
While the frogs hum their funny blues.

Clouds above are quite the jest,
Releasing laughter, oh what a fest!
WC and nature, a playful quest,
In puddles deep, we find our rest.

Join this splashy masquerade,
In every drip, life is relayed.
With every giggle, joy displayed,
Rainy days? A laugh parade!

Nature's Lull

Whispers of water, a cheeky sigh,
Giggling streams beneath the sky.
Tickling leaves as the breezes fly,
In this concert, joy is nigh.

Flowing like jokes on a Monday morn,
Sparkling laughter, bright and worn.
Misfits dancing, none forlorn,
In a river's jest, new tales are born.

The pond reflects a smile so wide,
Fish are flip-flopping, full of pride.
Nature's humor, it cannot hide,
Here in the laughter, we all abide.

When splashes echo, let's unite,
In nature's lull, everything feels right.
Join the fun, it's pure delight,
In this world, let's share the light!

Chorus of the Clouds

Fluffy guardians with a wink and a nod,
Dancing around like a merry squad.
With each drop, they give a prod,
Sprinkling joy on every sod.

Echoes of chuckles from high above,
As rain showers down, a friendly shove.
Bouncing raindrops, tales of love,
Nature's laughter, life to shove.

Caterpillars wear rain hats, it's true,
While worms wiggle in naught but dew.
In puddles, the world's a crazy view,
Who knew the sky could act so blue?

With splashes grand, here comes the cheer,
Creation sings, laughter to hear.
Join in the mirth, let's persevere,
In the chorus of clouds, nothing to fear!

Melodies in the Garden

In the garden, hoses dance,
Spraying plants with a sassy glance.
Giggling blooms with a wet parade,
Nature's jesters, memories made.

Running water, a playful race,
Squishy shoes in the muddy space.
A sprinkler's spin, a joyful flail,
Chasing rainbows, a giddy trail.

From tiny pots to giant beds,
Chirpy frogs in their water threads.
Laughter ripples, leafy shields,
While puddles jiggle, laughter yields.

And if you trip, oh what a scene,
Splashes fly, all in between!
Absurdity in every drop,
In this garden, fun won't stop!

The Serenade of Drips

Inside the watering can's spout,
Water drips with an air of clout.
Each drop holds a tiny tune,
Like a performing, saucy moon.

A tiny bird joins in the show,
Sings along with a chirpy whee-oh!
As I forget where I should spray,
Plants soak up my little ballet.

The bucket splashes, oh what a sight,
Water's ballet, pure delight!
Splashing colors, a vibrant quirk,
As critters dance and nature twerks.

A chorus of giggles, drops on skin,
Just a day full of playful din.
I'll laugh and splash till evening's glow,
In this parade, I'll steal the show!

Harmony of the Hidden Dew

In the early morning light,
Dewdrops giggle, oh what a sight.
They sway like singers on the grass,
Ready to make the chill pass.

Each droplet hides a story dear,
Of cheeky bugs who wandered near.
They giggle when the sunlight beams,
And sprinkle dreams in moonlit streams.

A garden dance, a playful waltz,
With tumbles, turns, no faults!
As I trip o'er my own two feet,
Mother Nature plays the beat.

In the glow of dawn, they drop and sway,
Oh, what fun they have today!
With laughter in every gleaming dew,
Nature's joke just for me and you!

Flowing Notes of Renewal

In the creek, where wildthings play,
Water flows in a jazzy way.
Bubbles pop like silly tunes,
Making ruckus under the moons.

Squirrels scamper, splash around,
Breaking beats without a sound.
Each ripple joins in the jest,
A nature's song, from east to west.

Jugs and jigs in wet ballet,
Splish-splash antics on display!
Water sings in whirly bends,
Off the jokes, the splashes send.

With each splash and playful roar,
The creek giggles, wanting more.
A symphony of joyful cheer,
Every droplet holds a dear!

The Quiet Anthem of Earth

In the garden, plants do sway,
Giving leaves a fun ballet.
A tickle here, a splash to there,
Nature laughs without a care.

Tickling roots with gentle streams,
Frogs join in with silly screams.
The daisies dance in soft delight,
As raindrops giggle, what a sight!

With every drop, a joke is told,
The soil laughs, both brave and bold.
Worms are wriggling, having fun,
While droplets wink, their work is done.

When clouds break forth and rains descend,
The earth and sky, a playful blend.
In choruses of joyful cheer,
Each splash is music, loud and clear.

Melodic Flow of Memories

A pot of daisies sings with glee,
As droplets bounce like balls of spree.
A little sprout, it shakes and laughs,
With thirsty roots, it takes the gaffs.

A butterfly, quite out of breath,
Dances near, forgets his quest.
And ants march by, a troop on parade,
While puddles form a splashy shade.

The tomatoes giggle, red and bright,
Sharing secrets in the light.
With each splash, old stories wake,
Of growing dreams and pies to bake.

As evening falls, the crickets croon,
Underneath the glowing moon.
In gardens where laughter can be found,
Memories sprout, joy unbound.

Whispers of Glistening Drops

Raindrops tickle each crooked leaf,
Frogs play tag in joyful brief.
Each ripple sends a chuckle 'round,
As puddles form beneath the ground.

A curious snail, with a shiny trail,
Decides to join this jolly gale.
He twirls and spins, then starts to slide,
On slick paths where giggles abide.

The flowers gossip on cloud nine,
Swapping tales with a splashy line.
Each droplet brings a twist of fate,
As nature hums and celebrates.

While sunbeams break the water's hold,
A rainbow's smile begins to unfold.
In the garden, laughter reaps,
As whispers of joy dance in heaps.

Serenade of Sprouting Greens

Oh, the broccoli is quite absurd,
Playing peekaboo without a word.
Lettuce twirls when rain comes down,
Each leaf adorned with nature's crown.

Carrots wobble in the dirt,
Wishing they'd grown a spiffy skirt.
The radishes, in rosy hues,
Play pranks and wear flamboyant shoes.

Tomato vines, like vines of rhyme,
Strut about, keeping perfect time.
Each drop's a note in green's refrain,
A symphony of humor in the rain.

The sun peeks through with a cheeky grin,
As earthworms twirl and join the win.
With every sprout, a laugh will please,
In nature's show, we dance with ease.

Crescendo in the Garden's Growth

In the plot where greens arise,
Basil chats with sprightly flies.
Tomatoes bounce, they twist and shout,
While carrots dance, and peas pout out.

With every splash, the daisies grin,
They sip and giggle, having a win.
Oh, see the potato take a leap,
And cabbage joining in with a sweep!

The sunbeams cheer from way up high,
As petals laugh and clouds pass by.
We'll host a ball, a garden show,
Where rain and lettuce steal the glow!

So bring your friends, both worms and bugs,
For leafy tales and playful shrugs.
In the garden's merry spree,
It's all about the botanic glee!

Waves of Nurturing Waters

When raindrops fall, they play a tune,
A splashy giggle, a watery swoon.
The flowers sway, they love the beat,
A rhythmic dance on nature's street.

In puddles deep, the frogs decide,
To surf the waves with glee and pride.
While slugs slide by with slimy trails,
Creating art beyond the gales.

With each droplet, plants start to cheer,
As squirrels dance, their tails in rear.
A sprinkler spins, like it's got flair,
Making rainbows in sunny air!

So come and join this zany ride,
Where veggies clap and seedlings glide.
In every splash, a laugh resounds,
In nurturing waves, pure joy abounds!

Whispers of the Verdant Revival

In secret shades, the leaves declare,
Their whispers dance upon the air.
'Cabbage crunch' and 'peashoot cheer',
They giggle softly, all sincere.

A dandelion winks with glee,
As ants march by, their bands agree.
The sunflowers strut in golden rows,
While gentle breezes tickle toes.

With every mist, the roots awake,
The lettuce dreams of leafy cake.
And in this patch, the world's alive,
A wondrous place where all things thrive.

Through leafy laughter, the garden speaks,
Of all the joy that nature seeks.
In verdant whispers, we all find a part,
A funny jest that warms the heart!

Rivulets of Joy

Drips and drops, a dance so spry,
Water plays like a giggling guy.
Splashing boots and squishy toes,
Who knew mud could be so close?

Puddles form for leaps and bounds,
Rubber ducks afloat in rounds.
Giggling streams like winding roads,
A symphony of squishy toads.

Buckets fly, and kids take aim,
Laughter echoes, it's all a game.
Hoses hose, and splashes spray,
Water fights make a sunny day!

With each drop, a giggle rings,
Nature's joke, oh, how it sings!
Rivulets twist, they play hide-and-seek,
Making us chuckle, week after week.

Lullaby of the Leaves

Rustling whispers dance with glee,
As droplets tickle boughs and trees.
"Hey, more rain!" the flowers shout,
While squirrels wear their raincoat clouts.

A leaf's a hat on a tiny head,
Water's laughter sparks joy instead.
With each drip, the branches sway,
Leaves giggle in their leafy ballet.

Puddles form in the garden fair,
As raindrops skitter everywhere.
Mice in boots enjoy their slide,
Sliding down on nature's tide!

So when the sky begins to weep,
Know that joy is yours to keep.
Listen close to nature's tease,
A witty tune in rustling leaves.

The Gentle Croon of Thirst

In a garden full of blooms,
Water whispers in the glooms.
"Drink up flowers, time to sip,
Join the party, don't you trip!"

Grass blades perk up, they prance about,
While birds chirp in a sunny shout.
Water falls in giggly splats,
Tickling earth beneath those hats.

A mischievous breeze plays around,
Spinning leaves in merry sounds.
In every droplet, joy abounds,
Laughter in the thirsty grounds.

So here's to quenching nature's thirst,
And all those giggles that come first.
With every splash, a jolly cheer,
A croon of joy for all to hear.

Crescendo of the Creek

The creek's a giggler, splashing wide,
As frogs in hats jump side to side.
"Come on in, let's take a dip!"
As feathery ferns start to flip!

A bubbling tune of water plays,
Making music on sunny days.
"Hey, crickets! Join our choir!"
A quack and then a splash of fire!

When sit down stones become our seats,
We share the laughter, tasty treats.
Fairies tease with drops of dew,
A creekside party, all askew!

Let water dance and plants now sing,
In this joyful, playful spring.
A crescendo of giggles, wild and free,
Nature's own raucous jubilee!

Chorus of Anticipated Blossoms

In the garden, giggles soar,
Every droplet seeks to explore.
Plants dance with a wiggle or twist,
Whispering secrets we can't resist.

Bunnies hop with giddy delight,
Splish and splash, what a funny sight!
Flowers chuckle in hues so bright,
Tickled by the morn's soft light.

Refreshing Tune of Fertile Grounds

A tap, a splatter, then a bloom,
Nature's prankster in every room.
Squirrels snicker at tiny rains,
While blossoms stretch and shake their pains.

Laughter echoes through the leaves,
As mushrooms dance like little thieves.
Each gust of wind, a giggling tease,
Entwining woes with joyful ease.

Aria of Nurtured Growth

Sprouts angle for a sunlit kiss,
"Hey, look at me!" they call in bliss.
Wiggly roots in a tangled play,
Singing nonsense as they sway.

With every drop that gets them wet,
They giggle 'til the sun can set.
A cacophony of glee unfolds,
As blooms erupt like cherished gold.

Resonating Raindrops and Tender Sprigs

Pat-a-cake on greens so lush,
Raindrops join in a happy hush.
Sprigs in line, they jive and prance,
Nature's stage, a wild dance chance.

Every splash a joke so fine,
Bamboo bends, in a wobbly line.
Laughter bursts beneath the sky,
As tiny critters waddle by.

Tender Sprigs

Giggles sprout beneath the mire,
Each plant dreaming of dance or choir.
Joyful murmurs fill the air,
As peas and carrots form a pair.

Ticklish tendrils wave with glee,
Making shadows, oh so free!
Nature's jesters, bold and bright,
Chase each other, pure delight.

Harmony of Lush Life

In the garden, plants have a chat,
With giggles and whispers, where they're at.
Roses tease daisies, 'Look at my bloom!'
While vegetables plot for the best room.

Bees roll their eyes at the ants so bold,
Saying, 'Can you believe? They think they're gold!'
Sunshine chuckles at the clouds in the sky,
As grass dances low, waiting to spry.

Inspiration from Nature's Gentle Flow

The stream's got a laugh, it's bubbly, it's bright,
With pebbles that splash, oh what a sight!
Frogs jump in tune, croaking their songs,
While turtles groove slow, never rushing along.

Butterflies flutter, they can't sit still,
Sharing their gossip, what a cute thrill!
They sip on the nectar, in joyful cheer,
Nature's such a hoot, how silly it's here!

Hushed Melodies of New Life

In the quiet of dawn, new sprouts wake slow,
Whispering secrets, in a soft flow.
A worm plays the flute, a snail hums a beat,
While the sun taps its toes on warm, sandy heat.

The raindrops can't wait for their turn on the line,
Dancing a jig on the old watering sign.
'Watch us,' they giggle, as they dive to the ground,
Each droplet a splash of laughter that's found.

The Cascade's Gentle Caress

Over rocks and round bends, the giggles cascade,
Water's making friends in a bubbly parade.
It slips, it flops, with a wink and a sigh,
Saying, 'Catch me if you can!' as it flows by.

Sprinklers join in with a spritz and a splash,
Turning the lawn into a waterway bash.
Kids squeal and jump as the droplets enhance,
A sunny day's laughter, a childhood dance!

Murmured Promise of Flourishing

In the garden, a jug did slip,
A gurgle, a splash – oh what a trip!
Plants laughing as they drink and sway,
While petals giggle, come what may.

A leaf wore droplets like tiny crowns,
While the soil danced in its muddy gowns.
Worms wiggled happily, pulling their weight,
As nature's party stayed up late.

Sunshine squinted at this uproar,
As bees buzzed loudly – they wanted more!
Each drop a note, each splash a song,
In this wet circus, you can't go wrong!

So grab your cans, it's time to play,
The flora's ready for the spray!
With laughter echoed, joy will rise,
In this bright world beneath the skies.

Nature's Refreshing Verses

Pitter-patter on the ground,
Plants all pirouette around.
A thirsty petunia shakes with glee,
As drizzles whisper, 'Dance with me!'

The daisies declared, 'We need a soak!'
And out came the hose with a jovial stroke.
Water's laughter filled the air,
While squirrels cheered from their high chair.

With a splash, the grass finds its groove,
While butterflies flit, right in the mood.
"Oh, look at that!" the daisies shout,
Mother Nature's mischief, no doubt!

Getting glistening was the aim,
But what's this, a garden game?
It's never dull when there's a spray,
Nature's fun show is here to stay!

Chorus of Liquid Embrace

A hosepipe sings, with rhythm and thrill,
Sprinkling smiles on the daffodil.
Pump up the volume, toss out the dread,
As water tickles the flowerbed!

The ferns in wild waltz twist and twine,
Under droplets that shimmer and shine.
Each petal catches a giggly drop,
As grass does the conga, never to stop!

Rain boots squelch, puddles like pools,
While splashes echo, ignoring the rules.
A ladybug joins, shaking her spots,
In this wet wonderland, fun never stops!

With each swish, the blooms feel alive,
In this joyful dance, they all thrive.
So come join the chorus, let spirits rise,
In this playful shower beneath blue skies!

A Song of Drenched Flourish

Raindrops jived on the windowpane,
A serenade of a wonderful rain.
Gardens twirling in their flamboyant coats,
While frogs locked arms and hopped like boats.

With a splash and a giggle, the daisies chime,
Every droplet, another punchline.
The tomatoes blushed, cheeks all aglow,
As they laughed at the lettuce doing the tango!

In this spongy party of lush delight,
Squirrels in slippers are quite a sight.
So grab your watering can, take a peek,
And join this soggy, silly streak!

Amid the green, there's joy and cheer,
Each splash a note, loud and clear.
So dance with the sun and let spirits soar,
In this growing laughter, forever more!

www.ingramcontent.com/pod-product-compliance
Lightning Source LLC
Chambersburg PA
CBHW070322120526
44590CB00017B/2789